Things We Say to Dogs
and
Other Four-Legged Observations

Written by: Lara Magallon

Lara Magallon
Carlsbad, CA 92009
lara@laramagallon.com

THINGS WE SAY TO DOGS

Dedication

To My Mother, Diane Dyer Street.

An email from my mother:

December 14, 2009

"Sure do miss all the wonderful Xmas days we shared and all of the excitement that we had together.

May God's love and light surround you and know that I miss you very much."

Blessings,

D.D. Street (Diane Dyer Street)

This book is dedicated to my mother and all of the animals that she helped throughout the years.

When she died, my brother Christopher was overwhelmed by the amount of solicitations for animal causes that she so selflessly supported.

Mom, you had so little, but gave so much…

I will now carry the torch you lit, protecting our precious animals.

I further dedicate this book to Paula, John Havens, Ken Fraser, Scott Hensley, Dr. Ben Singh and his wonderful staff at Aviara Animal Health Center, Dr. Proulx and the amazing staff at CVS Angel Care Cancer Center.

Lastly, thank you to all of the animal lovers of the world. It is through the kindness embedded deeply in our hearts that we can all make a difference in this life……

"Strong Souls Are Not Born They Are Built,

By Forging Through The Most Screwed Up Situations

And Still Having The Ability To Shine."

—Author Unknown, Facebook Post

Introduction

This book was inspired by the many conversations I have with "Granny," my crabby, white Jack Russell terrier. He likes to show us his awfully long and spiky teeth at night, just to remind us who is the boss in our house, especially when he's cranky.

He's eleven years old now. We are not sure how he made it this far. First, there was the close encounter with a car that ran over him.

Then he survived cancer.

The vet just needs a little more of our money and he can retire comfortably.

Granny endured three operations as the tumor grew back after each surgery. Our next step was to try radiation or to amputate his leg. So we took the less drastic route (depending on whether you ask me or Granny), and he underwent thirteen radiation treatments.

At the end of the radiation, Granny's leg resembled a half-cooked chicken thigh right off our wobbly barbecue.

Make no mistake: Granny had been cooked. But he's doing great now with just a pinkish area of healthy skin where the hair is stubborn and decided not to grow back.

Needless to say, because of Granny's ordeals, he gets tons of slack. He never misbehaves; it's always the other dogs.

Granny has a mind of his own, and nobody tells him what to do. He is as stubborn as a mule! It seems like every time we go for a walk, it is a battle of wills. If I want to go right, Granny wants to go left and vice versa.

One morning, some time ago, I came to a realization while standing on the curb, after telling Granny that we needed to turn around so I could get ready for work. It occurred to me that almost everybody talks to their dogs just like I do. So why not write a book about all the silly "Things We Say To Dogs?"

I'm always asked why I named my male dog "Granny." Actually, he started out as "Boomer." Granny is what we call him now. I'll talk about that later, since Granny is only a part of this story.

Others have shared with me the things they say and think about their wonderful dogs. So this book isn't all about Granny, but he will be our companion throughout this book for dog-lovers and animal-lovers, and I'll be telling his story too.

We picked Granny up from a rescue agency almost eleven years ago. Upon meeting Granny he made it clear there was no way he wasn't going home with us.

What we didn't realize at the time is that we picked up two Grannies': One who is nice during the day, then a wild snapping, fanged tooth Granny who appears at night. Just like in the horror movies. We got two dogs for the price of one.

"If there are no dogs in Heaven, then when I die I want to go where they went."

—Will Rogers

The Biggest Mule in Town

It is 6 am and I am busy yelling like a fool at Granny. I stand on a street corner trying to pull a two-ton mule that won't budge. We've already been walking for an hour.

"Granny, if you aren't ready to go back yet, then you are more than welcome to go to work on my behalf."

"You might do a better job!"

Granny isn't interested and keeps investigating the fake grass.

I wish I could stay home just like dear old Granny

and scratch while watching multi-colored insects flying by.

The Missing Turtle

🦴

The rock that you proudly brought into the house and dropped at my feet...

Is our missing turtle!

Little Red Riding Hood

My, what big teeth you have Grandma!

Granny is a very befitting name because of your protruding teeth that can barely fit in your mouth.

Just like the sneaky dog in "Little Red Riding Dog."

During the day you are a loving dog so you can get food and walks.

And then at night the mean grandma appears!

The Animal Human Bond

"People helping animals and animals helping people"

—Mike Arms, President, Helen Woodward Animal Center

Those Dopey Hillbillies

I see others driving around with a big dog plopped on their lap.

But when you start honking the horn, we look like a group of mismatched Hillbillies rolling into town in our fur filled, crappy, old Mustang.

All we are missing is hay in our trunk and chickens flying out of the windows!

The Infamous Pole

🦴

Hmmm...

We never seem to agree on which side of the pole we should walk.

The Flood

"Okay Pal, bath time!"

"Pal runs upstairs and hops in the bathtub, all 250 lbs of him, with an expectant look on his face."

"I could never get my kids to do that."

—Paula Magallon

Old Age Isn't for Sissies

What idiot said that for each year of a human's life, we need to add eight more to a dog's life?

When I rescued you we made a "paw shake" agreement you were going to prove that theory wrong,

And you were going to outlive me!

The Back End of a Chicken

You are as fast as the back end of a chicken that goes over the fence last.

And by the way, that ain't fast.

ROCKY

"Some say that dogs respond best to two syllable names… thus for 10 years now, we have owned 'Rocky'…"

"Repeating phrases seems to be quite comprehensible to dogs as well…."

"Thus, in doing his 'business', the commands of 'go', 'hurry-hurry' or 'go', 'slow-slow', seem to be followed with great precision."

"Our grandkids thought 'slow-slow' was a time out!"

—Chuck Butler, Lead Chaplain, Spiritual Care Services, Scripps Memorial Hospital, Encinitas

That Ain't No Stick!

You know the amusing stick you are trying to play with?

Take your ball and run for the hills...

It's a snake!

Full-Time Waitress

Do your dogs realize how lucky you are to have a full-time waitress at your "barking" call?

welcoming committee

"I am greeted by the best welcoming committee in town."

"A team of dogs."

"And each one is competing to see whom I will pet first."

—Marco L, on his Pomeranian Cody and Boxer Khloe

Hell's Bells

When I hear your little head shaking like a bell in the morning,

Are you telling me you are wide awake and ready for a walk?

Or is this your breakfast bell?

Life of Leisure

Why can't I have a life of leisure like you?

I see you lying about the house without a care in the world.

You casually walk around and sniff everything in sight.

It seems your full-time job is to recline on the lawn chairs or lay in the thick, green grass.

You have time to appreciate the small things, even the ants.

I have a brilliant idea…

Why don't I steer some of my problems over to you and you can manage them for awhile?

Our Beloved Pets

"We should all take lessons from our pets."

"Our pets don't judge; they have no ill will or animosity towards others and harbor no discontent."

"They are peaceful creatures and surround us every day with happiness and joy."

—Dr. David Proulx, DVM, Radiation Oncology, CVS Angel Care

Reading Magnet

You are a book magnet.

Why is it every time I take out a book to read?

You want to sit on my lap!

Let Me Live

"Let me live, and I promise you, I will do everything in my lifetime to project them."

"Mike Arms had been viciously attacked leaving him unconscious after rescuing a Shepard/terrier mix hit by a car in the Bronx. The injured dog that should not have been able to move licked him awake."

"He had an epiphany and made his commitment to both God and animal welfare."

"To his credit Mike Arms has saved more animals than any other person, dead or alive."

—Mike Arms, President, Helen Woodward Animal Center

Dumpster Diving with Bandit

Bandit is Granny's sister, also a Jack Russell terrier. We say she has a gland problem. She's a bit fixated on food, a true hunter/gatherer.

Bandit, I saw you jump in the trash compactor when you thought I wasn't looking.

Did you hear that loud crack while I was pulling you out?

That was my back!

You're too fat!

Take a piece of advice, if you ever go dumpster diving again.

First check out what you are jumping into and make sure you can get out on your own!

Home Is Where The Human Is

"Could I give up my pet if it meant getting into a homeless shelter and having a roof over my head? The answer is no, I love my dog Avery. She is my comfort, she listens to my problems. I could never imagine having to give her up because I was homeless."

"It would be the same as giving up my son to an orphanage. Avery is a part of my family. Pets give us unconditional love, companionship, loyalty, security and for the homeless warmth. Many people leave their pets at home or in yard tied up while they go to work."

"The pet is lonely, barks, and sometimes acts out by chewing garbage. To a pet, home is where the human is, it is not a place."

"It could be a tent, car, RV, motel room or a sleeping bag on the street; it doesn't matter as long as they are with their human family."

—Renee Lowry, Executive Director, Pets of the Homeless, Testimonial by a homeless veteran.

The Thanksgiving Turkey

Stop barking at the Thanksgiving turkey!

No matter how long you keep barking, the turkey is not going to fly off the counter and land in your kibble bowl.

Move on, Please

🦴

"Dak, why do you walk right in front of me at a much slower pace than everyone else?"

"And at 125 pounds there is no way to get around you!"

—Spencer Stein, our rescued Shepherd mix

Drunken Pirate

Is that you I see racing around the yard barking like a drunken pirate?

Don't you remember that I had a big fight with the neighbor over your barking?

I hear societal menaces like you fill up the police logs all the time.

You don't want to be entered into a police log, do you?

The Whites of Your Eyes

Peanut is number three in the pecking order, after Granny and Bandit. We think he's some kind of fuzzy little terrier mix. Very cute and cuddly, but the boy is afraid of his own shadow.

My, my, what huge eyes you have Peanut.

I can see whites in them, just like the full moon.

You must be on the way to the electric chair!

The Missing Crust

Gibby,

"Did you really think I was so stupid that I wouldn't notice that the apple pie was missing something important? The crust!"

"You are automatically guilty because you are the only dog able to jump on the counter."

"And on top of that, your mouth smells like pie!"

—Lauren M, shocked by her Pit Bull.

Middle of the Night

How could you possibly think that it's time to walk?

It's dark thirty!

Ever seen me walk around the neighborhood in my pajamas?

If I'm still in pajamas, that's a dead giveaway.

Take your leash and collar and head your tail right back to bed!

The Food Trough

Each one of you has your own dining style.

Peanut, you spit out the kibbles so you can eat the meat.

Granny, you stare at the food to see if it will jump out of the bowl so you can chase after it.

And Bandit, you vacuum up everything in sight.

Funny Dog

"You are such a funny-looking dog, it is a wonder anyone would be stupid enough to adopt you?"

"Well, I am that stupid person!"

—Jennifer Sohl, marveling at the unique appearance of her dog.

cookies

So...

"Are you claiming it was the scent of warm, chocolate chip cookies right out of the oven that justified the near-deadly incident you caused when stampeding down the hallway?"

—Tom

Cinnamon Bun

You look like a yummy cinnamon roll when you are curled up in the dog bed all warm and cozy.

The bed circles you like the crust and your body is the center.

Luckily you ain't big and fat like a cinnamon roll because you have a nice owner who walks you.

Remember that when you are looking for the next place to pee in the house!

The Puppet

You look like a puppet with your silly head poking out of the hole in the sheet,

Courtesy of when you were playing with that nasty looking ball.

Luckily for you,

I am crazy about puppets!

My Passion Is Animals

"The greatest thing I can do is to leave my mark on the hearts of all those I have touched."

"The same way a paw print was left on my heart."

"By the patients I have cared for over the many years of service."

—Dr. Ben Singh, DVM, Aviara Animal Health Center

The Traveling Dog Bed

Stop moving your dog bed all over the house!

Every day you transport it to a different location is a brand new opportunity for me to trip and break my neck...

And, if it's not too much to ask, leave the stuffing in!

The FBI

In the dog world, I must be a criminal under investigation by a scrupulous team of dogs snooping through my clothes and smelling my shoes.

Figuring out where I have been and whom I have seen.

Go join a local dog club or become a volunteer blood donor for "Pets of the Homeless."

The Greedy Grinch

Stop being the "Greedy Grinch" during Christmas!

Santa already broke the bank and bought you plenty of toys.

Why can't you let the other dogs enjoy their toys too?

Ever heard of sharing?

You have one toy dangling from your mouth while attempting to grab another.

And when I try to grab the toy that doesn't belong to you,

You drop it in order to seize another toy, ensuring your competition doesn't stand a chance.

The "Greedy Grinch" who stole Christmas has once again returned!

Nellie and Tillie

Nellie and Tillie,

"Why are you snubbing the buttered toast I am serving you for breakfast?"

"Is it because I didn't put enough peanut butter and jam on it for you?"

—D.D. Street, on her two Border Collies

Traveling Dog Hairs

Your white hairs travel everywhere.

They clear customs and board the airplane going overseas.

They get a free ride in my car while dangling from the ceiling.

My black and navy outfits are now a lovely shade of grey.

And even the washer and dryer have plum given up!

Thanks to you, I am wearing your fur coat every day of the week.

The Screen Door

"Feiffer, those horrible criminals that you sought to attack were our eighty-year-old neighbors hobbling with their canes, walking their pint sized Chihuahuas."

"Next time smash through the screen door, not the glass!"

—Kelly Mock, amazed at the destruction caused by his Dog.

The Disappearing Couch

"Brandy, how on earth did you manage to eat the entire couch in just one day?"

"When I left for work this morning, I had a couch."

"And when I returned it was gone!"

—Jana Cartier, shocked by her dog.

Dog Bed

There are millions of dogs who would love to have a soft, comfy dog bed.

So why do you keep destroying yours?

You must be some kind of a nut that needs to be committed to the "Doggie Asylum."

christmas snow

Are you aware your new toys serve two purposes?

One is to keep the toy box all filled up.

And the other is for the stuffing I use as Christmas snow to surround the decorations.

Did you ever glance up at the Christmas displays and notice something familiar about the snow?

Surprise! It's from all of your old toys!

sandals

Why didn't chew my crappy sandals from "Dog-Mart"?

Instead, you chewed my designer $3.99 work sandals missing their heels.

Mischievous Little You!

Ah-ha! I finally caught you in the act!

You didn't expect me to come home an hour early.

And lo and behold what did I see?

Your freshly mended dog bed being dragged into the living room once again and torn to shreds!

Dogs, Our Role Models

"We as humans should look to our dogs as role models, only then might we learn to share with each other, the unconditional love that our dogs share with us."

—John Solis, Agent, Nationwide Pet Insurance

New Right Arm

No worries.

I have another right arm to replace the one that you pulled right out of the socket.

I can just go pick one up at the local sporting goods store.

I hear that they come in all sizes!

The Cemetery

Announcing!

New bones delivered and buried daily in our backyard cemetery.

All that is missing are the tombstones.

Ever considered digging up someone else's yard?

Ricky

"Ricky you are so handsome."

—Loretta Berlonghi, recognizing what every poodle already knows.

My Shirt

Which dog turned into an upscale clothing designer?

My new blouse purchased at the thrift store is missing its sleeves.

There are shreds of the fabric hanging in your teeth and scattered throughout your dog beds.

If you are ever missing your bed and I am wearing a new shirt that looks like just like it,

You are not imagining things; I am wearing your bed!

The Escaping Jail Bird

Granny, how did John, the guy down the street, know your name?

I have never met John, but he sure seems to know you!

Now Steve is yelling "Hi, Granny!"

Who is Bill? And why is he calling to ask if I own a Jack Russell?

Granny, I didn't realize you knew more neighbors than I do!

The Ungrateful Growler

What evil monster possesses you to growl like an out of control grisly bear?

When I am trying to help your "tail" onto the couch?

Talk about biting the hand that feeds you!

Hurry up and Wait

🦴

What on Earth are you waiting for…Christmas?

The Broken Foot

Thank you ever so much for breaking my foot while trying to catch you.

You won't help an invalid and insist upon playing "hide and seek."

The minute I get close enough to grab you, off you go.

Just wait until I have two working feet again!

cast iron stomach

Apparently, you have a cast iron stomach.

You can eat anything at least ten years old, including things I can't recognize.

And you miraculously wake up the next morning looking just fine!

My Guardian Cooper

"I was in Costco Friday and asked Cooper (service dog in training) to remind me to get three bags of ice when we checked out."

"A man heard me and just smiled."

"I knew immediately that he talked to dogs too!"

—Leisa Tilley-Grajek, K9 Guardians, Founding President

Dog House

Tell me.....

Do you pay property taxes or a mortgage on your dog house?

Dirt, Dirt and More Dirt

Do I look like I need a second job?

You grace me with your presence on the newly mopped floor, your dripping wet toys filled to the gills with dirt and leaves.

How would you like it if you just spent one hour vacuuming your dog bed and I came marching in with muddy feet and stomped right on it?

The Maid Supervisor

Why are you continuously monitoring me while I am cleaning the house?

Will you write me up if I do a bad job?

How about fire me on the spot?

I will gladly toss you a mop and broom.

By the way, you have a fantastic built in "tail duster" that can be used for hard to reach cobwebs and spiders!

Fun and Games

I get it.

You deliberately toss all of your toys in the pool to see if I will fall in while trying to get them!

And if I do, you will laugh "until the cows come home."

The Screen Door

Checked your eyesight lately?

The screen door was closed and you went right through it, now we have a lovely hole.

And it's just your size and shape.

Big and fat!

Malo

"Malo was the only one who knew when I was hurt, sad or needed a friend."

"He was my companion and only friend I could count on".

— Eduardo Ramirez, MSgt, USAF (Ret), Founder OneVet OneVoice

Conscience Anyone?

Do you ever feel guilty about blaming another dog for a dogfight that you started?

Or stealing a ball from some unsuspecting dog and running home with it?

How about eating another dog's dinner when they weren't looking?

There's a New "Dogh-Nut" in Town!

Hey, have you ever heard of the new kind of "Dogh-nut?"

Who ever thought of that is quite a genius.

I hear they are quite tasty too!

Pee carousel

Around and around we go.

How do we get off the ever rotating "pee carousel"?

You mark it, and we clean it up.

Your dog tag says you live here,

So why do you need to keep proving it?

Maniac Bath

Can you tell me why you high tail it out of the house right after a bath like your tail is on fire?

Immediately rolling into something horrible!

Couldn't you have rolled in a flowerbed instead?

All I know is…

I ain't sitting next to you for a solid week!

The Endless Ball

If you want me to play ball all day long, I need to order a second set of arms from Sears, Or buy an automatic ball-throwing machine.

You Are Strange Looking

Ricky,

"Did you know that your face is longer than your legs?"

"How do you Wiener dogs manage to walk with two-inch legs holding up a twenty-pound head and not trip under it?"

—Carol Richardson, on her Weiner dog

The Vet

Why is it whenever we go to the vet's office, I can't pull you out of the car?

You plant tree sized roots in the seat, fiercely cling to the steering wheel.

Every time I pull harder, you get heavier and heavier!

Give me one good reason…

Why you growl at the vet like a wild animal?

Last time I checked the vet wasn't an ax murderer!

The Church of the Barking Sun

A small group of us hold church services in our homes and rotate them between us. Granny seems to always know when it's our turn.

What possesses you to become absolutely unruly while I am trying to conduct the church service at our house?

You greet people at the door and watch them sit down.

You bark during the meditation.

You won't let anyone listen to my lesson.

Now you are playing ball with them?

Not one of them is paying attention, and quite frankly, I don't blame them.

Furlough

"Seriously, calm down. Stop acting like this is the first dog you've ever seen."

"These people are going to think I never let you out of the house."

—Tom

Goodwill

If you don't start acting like a good dog, I will be donating you to "Dogwill"!

Maybe they can help.

No one else has been able to.

A Big, Fat Surprise

I am convinced you wear a watch

Or have a built in timer that goes off like the oven

Whatever timer you have

It must tell you the time for walks, dinner, and those ever important extracurricular activities,

Such as playing ball or eating treats.

The Rain Game

"Both of us can't fit under the umbrella, since you have more legs than I do."

"That leaves you out!"

—John Stillwell, on his Poodle

Tranforming Dog

Do you have some formula that I don't know about?

How do you magically transform yourself from a two-foot dog during the day into a giant seven-foot dog at night?

There's no room for me, not with you hogging the blankets and stealing my pillows.

And on top of that, I get awarded a generous two inches of bed,

Outside of the covers no less...

The next morning you wake up all refreshed and I look like a rotting old mummy who died long ago.

A ROCK

How are you going to possibly make it home carrying a rock twice the size of your head?

You can't possibly push it the entire way can you?

Now we have another beautiful rock adorning our yard, along with the million other rocks you have collected.

Granny's Going to Town!

Bandit, why are you licking Granny's entire face?

He looks like he just took a bath.

Granny must have told you that he was going to have another surgery today.

Who says dogs don't have feelings?

The Dead Toy

Oh no!

I hear the merciless shaking of a toy that will soon be dead and heading my way,

With you still attached, all ready to play!

Reveille

"Reveille, you are my life!"

"When I found out you had lymphoma, my world stopped. I couldn't snap my fingers and make the disease go away. The thought that I could lose you was more than I could stand."

"It was that moment, I decided to not let grief destroy me or the time I had with you, inspired me to form CLEAR".

—Terry Simons, President/Founder, Canine Lymphoma Education Awareness And Research.

The Ceiling Light

How did you manage to turn on the ceiling light in the car?

I wasn't aware you were tall enough to reach it.

Punctuality

🦴

What on earth do you dogs have to be punctual for?

Except for food, walks, and toys at Christmas.

You snob

Can you tell me what's wrong with your food?

It's all spiced up with fake bacon bits, prepared by a master chef from Tijuana, flown in by skateboard.

Next time you don't feel like eating, tune into "Wild Animal Planet,"

In case you haven't noticed, there are tons of hungry dogs in the world!

Keeping up with the Joneses

I was wondering,

Do you dogs compare your lifestyle, or lack of it, to the other dogs in town?

Such as, who has a statelier doghouse, a nicer collar, better toys, a more comfy dog bed, or a sportier car to be seen in?

Shasta

"Shasta, these treats are for you to chomp on during the day."

"Then I hit my head on them at night because you tucked them under my pillow."

—Laural Davis, on her Siberian Husky

Trapped in the closet

Why didn't you destroy the old robe when you got stuck in the closet?

My new silk robe hanging on the back of the door is filled with a zillion bite marks.

That was really smart of you trying to open the door with it.

If you find yourself caught in the closet again, turn on the light and check the label.

And if it's expensive, leave it alone.

Then grab something cheaper to chew instead.

Dinner

🦴

Couldn't you tell that the innocent little coyote you were playing with had a vision of you in between two dog slices of bread?

The Cover Thief

You have all the fur, so stop stealing the covers!

Sweet Little Eyes

You have the sweetest little eyes telling me that all is well with the world....

Even if I am a mess, you ain't!

You Are Perfect!

I wish more people would be more like you.

You don't give a rat's rear end if I am a wrinkled old prune with a nest of gray hair, or someone with a terrible facelift.

It doesn't matter to you if I have the newest hair style in town,

Or if I am wearing third hand "Dogmation Army" clothes.

In your eyes, I am perfect.

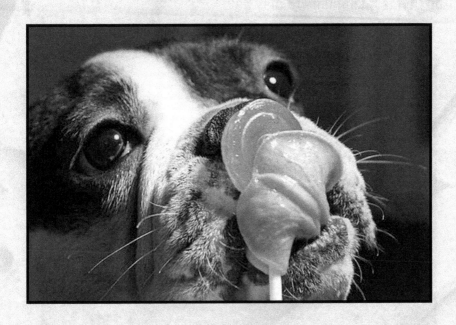

The Wet Ball

Well, who is that proudly trotting into the bathroom with the wet ball?

How can I be irritated at you when you look so cute?

We have to keep our little secret that you keep dipping the ball into the pool and bringing it into the house to play.

You made my morning special and made me realize what is truly important.

And that is taking time to play ball!

The Trash Trail

"Glad I finally caught you red-handed."

"I knew it was you who tipped over the trash!"

"You are like a little mouse dropping a trail of trash leading right to your bed."

"If you ever want to pass the buck, direct the trash towards another dog's bed, not yours!"

—Jana Cartier

Party Crasher

What are you doing, bouncing off the walls and announcing your presence to all the guests?

I didn't see your name on the guest list.

You are jumping and stomping around the room like a convict just released from prison.

Glad everyone else thought that you were amusing.

I sure didn't!

The Ninety-Nine-Cent Turkey Dog

Stop drooling at the barbecue grill.

The biggest turkey dog has my name on it, not yours.

You can settle for the smaller one because you don't pay any rent here.

There are plenty of dogs who never get a hot turkey dog off the grill.

Instead, they settle for some year old moldy kibbles.

Sleeping with the Enemy

"Who can sleep with that awfully busy mouth of yours gnawing all night long?"

"You are coming unglued."

"All the ferocious chewing, scratching, and shaking the bed, like the San Francisco earthquake."

"Oops! It must be flea season again."

—Ryan Mock, on his Jack Russell

The Walking Carpet

"Chubs, you look like a walking piece of second hand carpet."

"You are shaggy and brown."

"It is often impossible to find where you and the carpet meet."

"And it's even worse at night!"

—Lucy Faustino, on her mixed breed dog.

A Fair Fight

For a change, why don't you pick a fight with a dog your own size?

The German Shepherd you are growling at is four times as big as you.

With an even meaner looking owner following right behind!

A Pound of Bacon

Tony,

"Do you happen to know anything about the pound of bacon that disappeared off the kitchen counter?"

"Did you see anyone breaking into our house?"

"I didn't think so."

"And thank you so much for throwing up the slices whole."

"They are ready for the frying pan, to serve to our unsuspecting guest."

—D.D Street, on her poodle

Water, Water, Everywhere

How can you possibly be so thirsty?

You have only been in the car for five minutes!

Thanks to your drinking etiquette,

It looks like it rained inside, and the seat looks like I forgot to wear my extremely stylish Depends underwear.

Relocation Specialist

Was that you I saw down the street taking applications for a new home?

Be sure to take your leash and dog bed.

Before you hang your shingle somewhere else, check out the amount of walks you will get compared to mine.

Ain't No Fool

Apparently, you came to visit for just one night "to see if you could get along with the other dogs."

Three years later and you still haven't left.

Pat yourself on the back, because you outsmarted a house full of well-educated people!

Stuffed Animal

Peanut, with your scraggy fur here, there and everywhere,

And your beady little eyes blending into one ridiculous looking fuzzy head,

You look like one of Granny's old stuffed teddy bears.

The Pumpkin

How many times do we need to go back to the neighbor's yard to make sure that pumpkin isn't a ball?

The pumpkin belongs in their yard, not in your mouth!

You have already dragged me back to the same house three times!

What does it take to convince you?

TWO Dogs

I am positively convinced there are two different Grannies living here!

One Granny who moments ago, was fast asleep under blankets and pillows,

And the other Granny just appeared, standing in the kitchen all ready to eat.

Which Granny are you?

The Bed Volcano

🦴

"What happened to the new comforter?"

"Did you drag it out to the yard and bury it?"

"Or give it away to a homeless dog?"

—Lucy Faustino, on her mixed breed dog.

Life and More Life

In your wilder days, you ran, not walked.

You never had the time to notice small things, like how tall the trees are,

Or, the color of the roofs on the houses,

while the sun is coming up....

And strange-looking people getting their newspapers in the morn-ing, wearing even stranger-looking outfits....

Or our footprints in the dewy grass,

Now that we are both old farts, we have time to notice all of life's beauty.

While I am hobbling around with a cane and you are in a stroller!

The Carpet Cleaner

Can't you hear all that yelling while Tom is vacuuming the house?

You aren't imagining things!

And everywhere he goes, he gets madder and madder at you as he finds more of your messes.

If I were you,

I would be hiding under the bed too!

southside Dog

"Why am I always the "lucky" one to get stuck smelling the back end of a north bound dog?"

—Uncle Silas Edder, on his rescued Greyhound

My Service Animal

"I cannot express my gratitude to Pets of the Homeless, their quick and decisive action saved my Service Animal who is more like my child. I cannot tell anyone who has not experienced the feeling of isolated and helplessness, when your beloved pet is so sick."

"You feel so disgusted that you do not have the resources to provide the lifesaving attention they need and you do everything you can possibly do and you realize time is running out for them.

Then you get a call back.

And find out that indeed although you are one of the "invisible people", others look at but don't see you, as though you don't exist or perhaps prefer if you didn't. Pets of the Homeless will help you."

—Renee Lowry, Executive Director, Pets of the Homeless, Testimonial by a homeless veteran.

The Store

Good God, what are you doing running from aisle to aisle inside the grocery store?

Dogs don't belong in stores, they are for people.

The store clerk is trying to help me catch you and you are running around like a maniac.

How did you fit through the small opening I left in the window?

The Gas Pedal

Am I imagining things?

Every time I return to the car, you are wedged right in front of the gas pedals, right where my feet belong.

Unless you move, we ain't making it home for treats.

The Wonderful Ball

How did you know that I needed to be filled up with joy?

You and your tattered old ball

Roll right into town just when I need it!

Tractor and a Ton of Bricks

~

It must be wild, old, you crashing through the bedroom door, sounding like a tractor hauling a ton of bricks on its way to Texas.

I won't be surprised one day if you knock the door off the hinges!

The Adventures of Kelly and Fan

"Kelly, stop chasing after the man with the bag! I can't hold you anymore!"

"You are too strong!"

"I then proceeded to perform a back flip in my nylons, skirt and high heels, with my fanny landing right on the pavement. Luckily, Fan the other boxer with me didn't "strong arm" me and run off!"

"A lucky man, who had witnessed this whole ordeal, helped me to my feet, kidding me that "I needed a third dog to walk!"

" We both laughed so hard we cried."

—Carol Dax, on her two boxers

The Couch Monster

Why are you growling at me like I am stealing your toys when I am trying to help you up on the couch?

I have much better things to do than help a crabby old dog.

Mean dogs are welcome to sit on the cold floor!

Dog Court

There must be a court system for dogs, so they can testify against one another and settle barking issues, street fights, and toy stealing.

If there were such a thing, you would find your tail in court every week.

Special Dog Thoughts

"To love a dog and see it through life, all the way to old age and its accompanying frailties is indeed a blessing."

"It is an opportunity to experience pure love—both given and received—and in learning to speak through the heart."

—Lisa G. Murray, Marketing/Public Relations Director, HandicappedPets.com

Paw Prints

Mopsie,

"Eventually I will find you; I just need to follow the trail of your wet paw prints!"

—Jeannette D'Arcy, on her mixed breed

The Running Terror

"Why are you are running around the house like a dog late for work?"

"Except you don't work, so what's the rush?"

—Lauren M, shocked by her Pit Bull.

The Dog Fight

Why do you start a dogfight while we are crossing a busy street?

Can't it wait until we make it the other side alive?

Apparently not, since you manage to do it every time we walk.

One of these days, the cars won't stop and we will all be pancakes.

Followed

You don't need to keep turning your pint-sized head to look back every two seconds to see if the mean old coot is still walking behind you.

I am!

The Little Puppy

Even though you are as old as the hills,

You once again, become a little puppy racing through the long blades of grass.

Warming my heart as I watch you!

Walking Three Dogs

The three of you have your own places to go, and each one of you yanks me in an entirely different direction.

Why can't we all try to go the same way?

Oh how much fun it is to have all of the leashes tangled up into a big fat rats nest.

And I am caught in the middle struggling to get free.

Now we have to go home to get me "unstuck!"

The Rainy Day

Why on earth do you want to walk in the pouring rain?

Go take a peek, ain't no other dogs are out there.

But off we go anyway!

And our umbrella refuses to cooperate, and flips upside down, and now we are drenched.

I hope you're happy now!

Bad Medicine

Didn't you listen to the on oncologist?

The nasty tasting pill that I am unsuccessfully hiding in your food is supposed to help cure you.

So stop eating around it or the veterinarian will be having a little "bark" with us!

Babies

❖

"You are my little babies, all members of my precious family."

—Julia Luna

The Ball That Got Away

Why are you bent over like a pretzel, paddling the water in the pool?

What are you after?

Oh! I see!

You are trying to pull your tattered old tennis ball closer to you so you can play with it.

God's Gift of Balls

Today God must have thrown you another new ball from heaven.

Every time you are heading for surgery, you find a new ball.

That is three times now!

In just a few hours, you will be operated on once again.

And your new ball will be waiting for you.

Along with me!

The Burglar

Unless there's a fire or a burglar in the house, don't bother me.

We always seem to have a lot of burglars when I'm trying to take a nap on Sunday.

My Special Dog

"My dog loved me."

"He was always happy when I came home, he would follow me everywhere".

—Eduardo Ramirez, Founder, One Vet One Voice

The Pool

Why don't you believe me when I tell you that you can't possibly lick all the water out of the pool?

Special Toys

Out of all your new toys, what makes this one so special?

Pity the fool who tries to get near it.

Sooner or later they will be missing a paw.

The Dog Crew

🦴

When one of you follows me to the back yard,

I am guaranteed that the whole dog crew is just a few paws
behind.

W-A-L-K

"I spell w-a-l-k if we are not ready to go right away."

—Kerry Powell

The Mystical Leaves

I could never understand your fascination with the gutter,

Until I stooped down to see why.

It's the leaves that you are trying to catch as they float down the street.

I hope that you have better luck with them than the birds you chase!

Tyler's Little Fuzzy Bathrobe

"Tyler, you are my little man in a fuzzy bathrobe," talking to his little Yorkshire terrier.

—Dr. Ben Singh, DVM, Aviara Animal Health Center

The Delicacy

I watch you ever so delicately choose which toy you want to play with.

Just like a piece of fine candy that has been double dipped in white chocolate!

Dismembered Toys

The house is filled to the brim with all sorts of dismembered toys.

The victims are a headless doll, an octopus missing its tentacles, a bee without an eye, and a bear without a nose.

Nope, nothing strange-looking about these toys!

Times Are A-changing

🦴

Did your internal dog clock inform you daylight savings time is over?

Let's see if you can herd my big rear end out the door for a walk at the new time or the old time.

Nosing Around

The glass front door is covered with your wide array of nose marks.

Are you signaling to the dogs outside that you are a hostage?

our Veterans

"It is an honor for us at Kuranda Dog Beds to donate our beds for the support dogs our VETS so vitally need."

"This is something we look forward to every year."

—Mike Harding, Owner, Kuranda Dog Beds

Good Vibrations

How can you possibly be so happy all the time?

What kind of medication did your psychiatrist prescribe?

Maybe I should take it!

Dog Disorders

I have all three of you neatly categorized in my "dog database".

Peanut, everybody scares you, and you have panic attacks riding in the car.

Granny, you can't sit still long enough to take a breath.

Bandit, you howl and cry if we leave you alone in the house.

Congratulations, the three of you are as nutty as Aunt Agnes' fruitcake that nobody eats!

Treats

🦴

"Treats-o-rama for everyone!"

—Loretta Berlonghi, on her beloved poodles.

House Arrest

On the weekends, I have three proud members of the dog-law enforcement team following me whenever I go.

You make sure I can't slip out of the house without taking you for a walk or a car ride.

If I try to go out to the front yard to check the mail, my GPS tracking ankle bracelet goes off.

Oh! That's you, Peanut, nipping at my ankle.

Sun God

Let's see, you have baked in the sun for forty-five minutes.

It's time to roll over and bake on the other side for even browning.

Plan on doing any chores today?

Granny the Werewolf

Granny, you would make an excellent werewolf.

At night, you turn into a fanged wild creature snapping, biting, and growling.

Strangely enough, the next morning the mean werewolf has transformed

Into an awfully nice Granny standing at the door all ready to walk.

Food Snob

Whenever I have something yummy to eat like ice cream, you become my best friend in town!

Earlier in the day while eating eggs and spinach with low-fat cottage cheese, you were nowhere in sight!

My Royal Empire

My Dachshunds are a small Royal Empire of sorts.

"Murphy" is the King and protector of the kingdom. A strong leader and lets everyone know it. So I say… "You do know who the real King is around here, don't you?" He looks at me with those big brown eyes, like, "yeah, me!"

His sister is the Princess "Sweeny" and a warrior in her own right. I say to her, "How can you be so sweet and yet so aggressive?" She just smiles sheepishly and says, "oh, not me."

And finally the Royal Prince, "Gunner" is super spoiled with looks that would melt butter in a heartbeat. When I say "Get the ball" he is up a wagging and ready to play, play, play! Sometimes I think he's just the court jester.

—Ken Fraser, Impact Book Designs, on his Dachshunds

The Television Set

Apparently, the glass front door is your version of cable TV and a source for the local news.

You park your rear in front of it, staring out all day long, breaking only for water and food or god forbid a "barking alert."

My Most Faithful Friend

"It would be hard to find a friend more faithful or attentive than my dog!"

—Kris Rising, Owner, Pioneer Rock & Monument

Jack Russell Rescue

I rescued you from the Jack Russell Rescue Organization.

What you didn't know at the time

Is that you rescued me!

Peg Leg

🦴

The oncologist fibbed when he said your hair would grow back!

You still resemble a half-baked chicken or a peg-legged pirate.

Metal Bowls

I guess you wanted your new food bowl to look like your old bowl, so you chewed it up in no time flat.

Now I know why they make metal bowls.

For ungrateful dogs like you!

The Frozen Stare

Stop looking at me with the classic "frozen-dog stare!"

You never offered to share an ounce of your food, so don't make me feel guilty about not sharing mine!

Our Beloved War Dogs

"One of the best things we've done was to send out beds to Iraq and Afghanistan, to give the War Dogs a comfortable place to rest after putting in 18 hour days searching for IED's or whatever."

"The beds were sent under our donation program."

"We sent probably 50 beds to Iraq and 15 or so to Afghanistan."

—Mike Harding, Owner, Kuranda Dog Beds

Endless Smells

Why can't anything ever get by you?

Do you have to sniff everything in sight?

At this rate we will never get home.

Every few minutes we are forced to stop and sniff at something unrecognizable.

Can you tell me what is so important to know?

Dog Classification

Tell me,

As a dog, are you more of a "people dog" or a "dog's dog?"

Does that even make sense?

Home Is Where the Dog Is

I could be on some remote island or lost at sea.

If you are with me, I am home.

The Invisible Clock

Do you dogs have an invisible clock buried underneath your skin that I don't know about?

Every Saturday at 3 pm, you are waiting for a walk.

I can't even go near my shoes or sweatshirt.

And if I do, the three of you are lined up at the door.

Just like little Marines.

The Thinker

Don't matter if it is day or night, while going to the bathroom, you resemble a marble statue at Hearst Castle frozen in place.

The Vacuum

Why is it every time I vacuum, you change from a calm dog to a nutcase?

You bark until the vacuum shuts off or I get a headache, whichever comes first!

Are you protecting me from the "big bad vacuum?"

And if it's so dangerous, why you don't become a fearless dog and tackle this wonderful "vacuum" task,

So nobody in the house gets hurt!

The Long Arm of the Law

Everybody in the whole house positively trembles in their boots, when they see you walking around with your short, pointy ears and medium-sized tail, cracking your leash like a whip!

Santa's Reindeers

I look like Santa being pulled up and down the hills by an odd assortment of dogs, directly in front of me, like little reindeers,

All that's missing is the sleigh and an over sized red suit.

But not my fat stomach!

The Revolving Door

🦴

I must look like the stupidest door man to you.

In and out the door you go,

I am going to install a revolving door, just like the bank.

Instead of my revolving arm.

You Must Stay

Did you know that you are not allowed to get old and die?

You are supposed to live forever!

Dog Personalities

Some dogs resemble librarians because they detest noise.

While others dogs pretend to be star athletes displaying their running skills and ball catching abilities.

And other dogs act like growling gang members, hiding their tattoos under their fur.

However, most dogs are absolute loud mouths who annoy every neighbor in town.

Which category do you fit into today?

Nila Is A Great Little Shopper

"Recently, I had run out of peanut butter so we went to the grocery store together. (I put peanut butter in the "Kong" toy for Nila). While in the aisle I asked Nila,"

"Do you want chunky or smooth peanut butter?"

"Nila then touched the "smooth" peanut butter with her nose and that is exactly what we bought."

—Rachelle Christianson, K9 Guardians, PR, on her German Shepherd

Heaven

Promise me….

When you die I will come and visit you in Heaven.

You just need to tell me where you will be playing ball…..

The Patio-furniture Inspector

Doesn't the patio furniture meet your expectations anymore?

I see you inspecting it and checking out the paint.

I took the cushions off to clean them.

Find someplace else to take a nap.

Haircut from Hell

Did I overhear the other dogs in the neighborhood making fun of you after your haircut and bath?

Don't worry; it will eventually grow back after a ten years.

Meanwhile, just keep hiding under the bed!

Land of a Thousand Kibbles

Welcome to the "Land of a Thousand Year Old Kibbles."

Do you dogs ever wonder how a bowl full of kibbles appears twice each day?

Not by magic.

And no doubt, I will get written up if it's five minutes late.

A Dog Is A Great Listener

"A dog is more than a lover."

"A dog is a great listener and your best friend."

—Rickey, In memory of all of the men and women who served our country.

Horsing Around

You look so silly when you run,

Bobbing up and down like a horse on a carousel,

Up and down, up and down, round and round you go.

And where you stop, we'll never know.

Separation Anxiety

🦴

With you still attached to the ball, how can I possibly throw it?

Fido, My Best Friend

"We get our blessings from being on our knees."

"I miss my best friend Fido, regardless of how bad my day was, or times gone by, friends who would deceive me or whatever my problems were at the time."

"Fido, my best friend was always there for me."

—James Walton, retired Staff Sgt.

Dogs on Tables

〜

What idiot ever told you that dogs belong on tables?

The Pee Pole

Is there a magic number of times that you have to pee on the same pole?

You have made your point,

We all know you live down the street!

The Dog Escort

It's impossible to go anywhere in the house without my well trained security team trailing right behind, ensuring I am safe and sound while traveling from room to room!

Max My Rescue

"Max, your extraordinary love over the past ten years, has shown me the pathway to open myself up more deeply to the current of love."

—Nancy Priestly, on her mixed breed rescue Chihuahua

Popularity contest

I was just awarded the winning prize in the "old bat" popularity contest.

I received the most votes for walks, coming home from the "coal mine" on time, serving the best canned dog food ever.

What did I win? Oh, lucky me!

More dog walks!

The Dual Heaters

I am saving money with my dog heaters.

I have two small dog heaters on my right and left.

And a two-ton dog heater at my feet.

Dog heaters are so economical to run.

Fuel them up with dog food and water,

And they are good to go!

Toy Collection!

You must have brought every toy you own into the living room.

If there is a point to this, I can't figure it out just what it is.

You ain't suggesting you need more toys are you?

Tuck, Lucky, Sambo, Mason, Happy & Coco

"The English language is a beautiful thing."

"My best friend is GOD and man's best friend is his DOG."

"I give thanks to GOD for my DOGS (my best friends) Tuck, Lucky, Sambo, Mason, Happy and Coco."

"Thank you Jesus for our dogs."

—Christopher Huges Ellis, Owner, On 3 Say Cheese Photography

The Burglary Association

Since you are so familiar with everybody's schedule in the neighborhood thanks to your numerous walks, you can have a second career selling household information to the local burglars.

Nobody would suspect you because you look so small and innocent!

santa Claus Is coming to Town

I didn't know that Santa Claus came to town two months early.

Christmas is in December, and this is only September.

You have a bunch of white toy stuffing hanging from your mouth like Santa's beard.

Now all you need is matching white eyebrows!

Your Creative Couch

My, haven't you made yourself at home.

Looks like you made a creative couch on the ground by pulling down two pillows and the comforter!

Family Members

"Can you explain to me why you keep barking at the same family members returning home, night after night?"

—William Little, on his Lhasa Apso

Graham Crackers

Where on earth did my graham crackers and milk go?

I didn't imagine I put them out.

I came back to eat them and they disappeared.

The Barking Colony

I can only imagine what the neighbors are thinking with all of you positioned in various parts of the house barking at the top of your lungs.

Then for extra torture, you head out to the yard and bark.

I bet the poor neighbors wish we would pack up the herd and high "tail" it out of town!

The Pee Break

Dogs are lucky because they can go to the bathroom anywhere they feel like.

Tom sure was mad when I had to go, and we were sitting on the freeway in downtown Los Angeles stuck in mounds of traffic during rush hour.

Deflated Snowman

What are you doing sleeping on the snowman?

With your rear end planted right on him, I can't possibly blow him up for Christmas so he can join the other decorations!

The Household Manager

You walk around with such authority!

I imagine that you have a lot of responsibility, juggling all of the bills and household affairs.

No doubt it must keep you up at night!

The Big Enchilada

You look like the foot long enchilada that I order at my favorite Mexican restaurant, all folded up in the blanket with your furry white head poking out!

Fat Jack

⊶

"Jack, now that the vet has confirmed that you don't have a tumor, you have now run out of excuses to lose weight."

—Cynthia Magallon Puljic, on her Border Collie.

Pancakes

Since when are dogs allowed to help themselves to pancakes and syrup at the kitchen table?

Wise Dog Eyes

What do you see with your wise dog eyes?

Could it be… your owner's soul?

The New Ball

I see what is so fascinating.

It's your new ball lying at the bottom of the pool!

With a huge bite out of it!

Shear Luck & Bones Investigations, Inc.

The investigative agency of "Shear Luck & Bones" has opened up once again.

Both of you are taking endless notes while walking,

Inspecting the ground, the air, and the plants with your noses to make sure you haven't missed an important clue.

The Water Bill

If you like playing with the water so much,

Why don't I tape the bill to your bowl?

And you can pay it!

"Dogstroms" and "Doggy Marcus"

Won't I look chic holding you as a purse, going into all the snooty high-end stores that I never buy from?

Who knows?

I could be an upcoming member of the "Dogashian" clan!

Bad Breath

How could it be possible that your breath smells better than mine?

You don't even own a toothbrush!

The Property Tax Bill

I am going to put you in the mail and see if the tax collector would consider taking you instead of a check!

From what I spent on your radiation, I could pay my entire year of property taxes.

I hope the tax collector likes dogs.

Laundry Duty

"Do I have any volunteers for laundry duty?"

"Which one of you is going to be the lucky dog today?"

—Joanne Phillips, on her Boxer

The Dog Party

Tell me....

Can you possibly shed some light on which "dog party" you belong to?

Are you "Dog-publican," a "Dog-mocrat," or a "Dog-pendent?"

Whichever party you belong to must explain all of the big dog-fights I see in the streets!

The Coffee Table

"Owen, why didn't you chew all of the coffee table legs so at least they matched?"

"You only chewed two of them."

—Kelly Mock, on his Boxer

The Rescue Agency

Last time I checked, riding in the car doesn't mean I am returning you as "damaged goods" to the rescue agency.

Rats

You dogs are good-for-nothing cruisers.

Earn your keep; you haven't caught a rat in months!

Dinner

🦴

Who invited you for dinner?

Get off the kitchen chair!

The Circus

Why don't you join the circus?

You're just as talented as the other dogs!

You already have plenty of practice running around the pool just like a circus clown, jumping sky high while catching a toy.

The Wonder Dog

"Here comes the wonder dog!"

"Cutter would greet me with a stuffed toy in his mouth then run around the family room three times and come right back and drop the toy."

—Bill Lawton, on the best dog he ever owned.

Whisky Barrel

Bandit, Did anybody ever tell you? You are as fat as a whisky barrel?

DOGS ARE SUCH A BLESSING

"The animal species are life forms of God as are the human species. We are blessed by their presence."

"They serve humans well and provide guidance, direction, and literally teach through their magnificent presence and unconditional love, loyalty, living in the NOW, detachment, forgiveness, and integrity."

—Angelo Pizelo, President, Emerson Theological Institute

Molly

"Molly is my service dog for Wounded Warrior Homes. She is a big part of the healing that goes on here. I talk to Molly all the time and she rarely talks back…. But she speaks to me just the same."

—Gene D. Jennett, Assistant Director, Wounded Warrior Homes.

Laying an Egg

"With all of your legs underneath you, you look like you are laying an Easter egg."

—Jordan Mock, on his Jack Russell

The Grazing Cow

Are you sure you are not a distant relative of the cow family?

Peculiarly enough, You resemble a cow with your head tilted and your mouth busily vacuuming up every last bug in the grass!

Heater Seniority

Tell me, do dogs have some sort of seniority when it comes to sitting in front of the floor heater?

For example, do you go by which dog is the oldest or the meanest?

Dog Pillows

Oh, I see three dog pillows on the couch.

One small dog pillow on each end and an over sized dog pillow in the middle!

Exhausted

Why are you yawning?

You don't even work!

What on earth do you have to be tired about?

All day long you play with the toys or pretend to be a guard dog, barking at nothing important.

And that's when you find the time between naps.

Making the Bed

You lazy coot, get off the bed!

I can't make it around you!

My Underwear

Thank you for dragging my underwear right onto the patio where the pool man is working.

There is no way he can miss it, and there is no way I can hide it.

Mop Radar

You must have some kind of mop radar that I don't know about.

Every time I mop,

For one reason or another, you walk on the floor.

Can't you possibly wait until it dries?

The Witch's Broom

Isn't it funny to see our neighbor standing in the middle of the street?

All ready to chase us away with her broom.

Now all she needs to do is ride it right out of the neighborhood.

Curbside Escargot

Thank you so much for helping the city vacuum up all the snails and worms along the curbs and sidewalks.

Your walks serve two purposes:

Cleaning the sidewalks and saving money on food.

Ever met anything you couldn't eat?

walk on water

You can do no wrong.

I see you with rose-colored glasses.

The sun rises and sets on you.

Bless all of the very special dogs of the world.

You are one of them......

Backing up and Going Forward

Good God!

How many times do you need to keep backing up and going forward to make a run at the couch?

You'll never make it up there.

You must be a relative of the Goodyear blimp attempting to jump over the Cascades!

Dental Floss

Tell me…

Is this your inventive doggie version of dental floss?

You look hilarious with shreds of the tennis ball dangling from your fangs.

Dog Alarm

🦴

It's a three-dog alarm!

No one can get past such heavily armed dogs with tennis balls and toys!

Chicken Pot Pie

If you don't start behaving, you will end up in the chicken pot pie.

Hopefully, you taste better than you look!

The Transplanted Grass

Did you take time off from your part-time security job to study architectural magazines?

You must have, because the new turf that was once in the backyard is now inside the house, adorning the furniture, carpet, and tile.

Clearly marked with a dirt trail!

Green Movement

Are you a member of the "green movement"?

You must be, because you make a fantastic mobile garbage disposal and compact recycling plant!

Vacuum Power

Let's test out the power of the new vacuum.

You sit in front of it and we will see if I can vacuum up an eighteen-pound dog!

If not, we will return it, because the advertisement lied.

You Need a Facelift

Hey, have you seen your profile in the water bowl lately?

In case you didn't know it.

You are in dire need of a "muzzle lift."

You are all floppy, saggy and baggy with multiple double chins and a nose as long as a skyscraper!

The Dishwasher

How about a part-time dishwashing position?

I can get you to lick off all the dirty dishes, while saving money and tons of water.

I can kill two birds with one stone!

Pulling Teeth

Thanks to all the rocks and chew toys,

You have already removed the beehive of rotting teeth.

That the veterinarian suggested we yank out for **$500** dollars a piece.

Tumors

Didn't you hear the veterinarian telling us that he had heard of other dogs removing their own tumors?

So…why haven't you removed yours?

Catherine the Neighbor

🦴

Isn't it hilarious that our uppity next door neighbor Catherine?

Who has had way too many facelifts to count?

Never once complained about your barking while I was at work earning $1.25 an hour flipping loans.

Instead, she complained about our half-deaf and blind cat, Dudley, who could barely move.

Toys Everywhere

Those wonderful looking toys at the pet store are not free!

You can't scoop them up and head out the door.

Someone has to pay for them.

I assume you brought your "kibble" allowance!

The Streets

Last time I checked, dogs don't belong in the middle of the street!

The Air Bag

Good God,

Lose weight!

You are so fat, when you sit down in the passenger seat the air

bag blew up!

The Bark of My Heart

"We are the voices of our dogs and they give us unconditional love."

"Dogs are the bark of my heart."

— Carrington Kingsley, Owner & Pet Consultant, Kingsley Pet Sitting.

Dust Mop

When you lie down,

You look like a raggedly old dust mop that has seen much betterdays.

Itching to be tossed out on the curb!

The Circle of Life

"Our loving pets may leave us all too soon, but their memories linger in our hearts forever."

—Marguerite Johnson, Owner, Circle of Life Pet Crematorium.

My Doggy Stories

Use the space below to write about your own funny stories or memorable things that your beloved dog has done to fill your life with joy. It will be a wonderful keepsake for many years to come.

_____

_____

_____

_____

_____

_____

_____

_____

_____

_____

My Doggy Stories

My Doggy Stories

My Doggy Stories

_____

_____

_____

_____

_____

_____

_____

_____

_____

_____

_____

_____

_____

My Doggy Stories

_____

_____

_____

_____

_____

_____

_____

_____

_____

_____

_____

My Doggy Stories

_____

_____

_____

_____

_____

_____

_____

_____

_____

_____

_____

_____

_____

About the Author

Lara Magallon is an animal advocate and a former board member of the North San Diego County Humane Society. She holds a Masters degree in business management from University of Redlands, with a special emphasis on marketing, and a Ph.D. in Religious Studies at Emerson University. She is a volunteer Reverend at Scripps Hospital.

Lara Magallon
Carlsbad, CA 92009
lara@laramagallon.com

CPSIA information can be obtained
at www.ICGtesting.com
Printed in the USA
LVHW051114131118
596831LV00006B/606/P